DRAGONS

Cavendish Square
New York

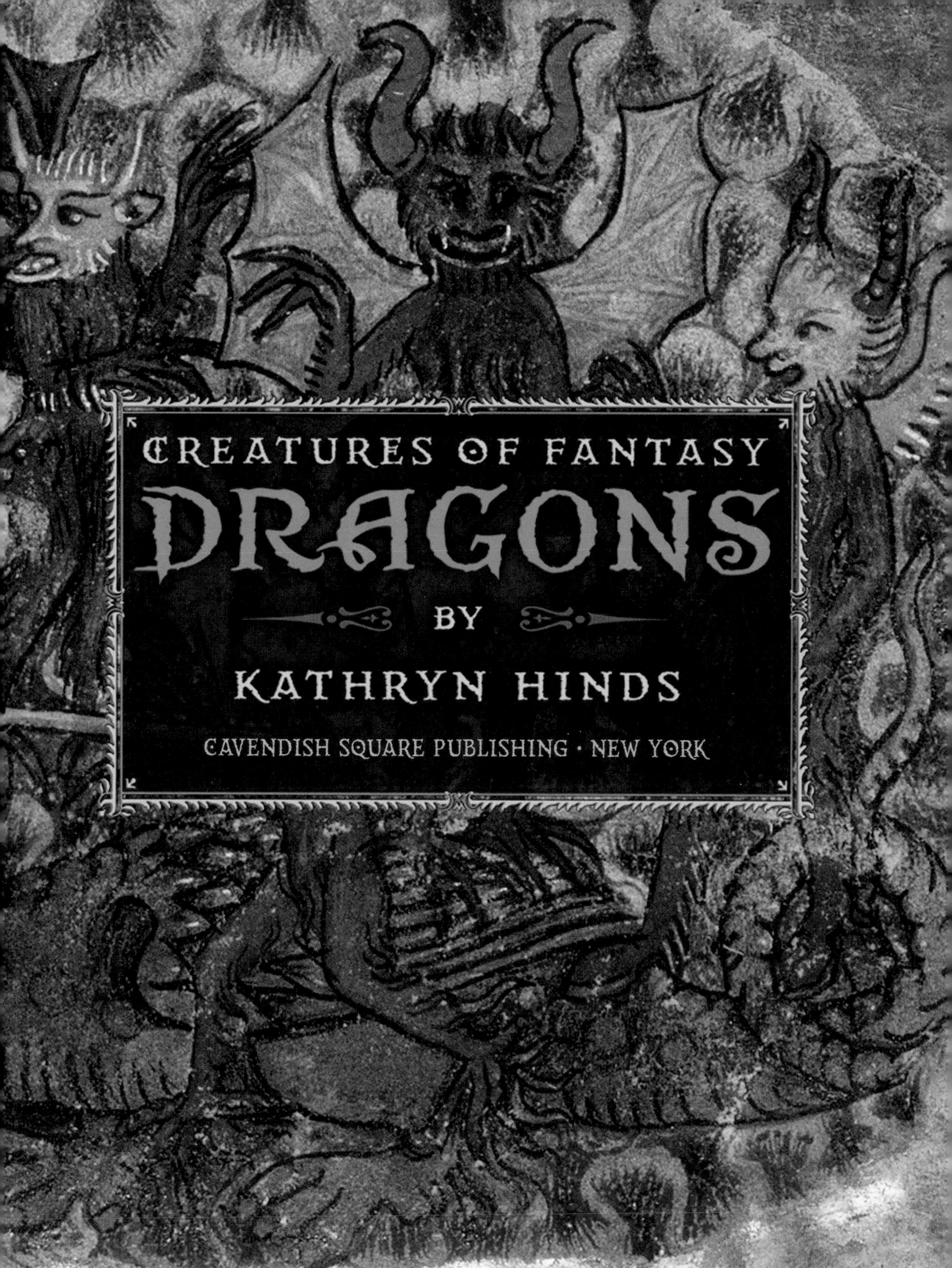

CREATURES OF FANTASY
DRAGONS

BY

KATHRYN HINDS

CAVENDISH SQUARE PUBLISHING · NEW YORK

For Sylvan

Published in 2014 by Cavendish Square Publishing, LLC
303 Park Avenue South, Suite 1247, New York, NY 10010

First Edition

LIBRARY OF CONGRESS CATALOGING-IN-PUBLICATION DATA

Hinds, Kathryn, 1962- Dragons / by Kathryn Hinds. p. cm.—(Creatures of fantasy) Includes bibliographical references and index. Summary: "Explores the mythical and historical backgrounds of dragons, both in the East and the West"—Provided by publisher. ISBN 978-0-7614-4920-1 (hardcover)—ISBN 978-1-62712-051-7 (paperback)—ISBN 978-1-60870-680-8 (ebook) 1. Dragons. I. Title. GR830.D7H628 2012 398.24'54—dc22 2010023597

Editor: Joyce Stanton Art Director: Anahid Hamparian Series Designer: Michael Nelson

Photo research by Debbie Needleman. The photographs in this book are used by permission and through the courtesy of: Front Cover: © The Bridgeman Art Library/SuperStock. Back Cover: © Hemis/Alamy. Page i: The Granger Collection, New York; pages ii-iii, 44: © The British Library/StockphotoPro; page 8: © Victor Habbick Visions/Photo Researchers, Inc.; pages 10-11, 36: © Bridgeman Art Library/Getty Images; page 12: © Bill Bachman/Alamy; page 13: © Francisco Cruz/SuperStock; page 14: © Charles Walker/Topfoto/The Image Works; page 17: © E. STROUHAL/Werner Forman/Art Resource, NY; page 18: Three-headed snake (wood), Indian School/Mumbai, India/© Dinodia/The Bridgeman Art Library International; page 20: © Joe McDonald/CORBIS; page 22: © Mary Evans Picture Library/The Image Works; page 25: © Cadmus and the Dragon, Zuccarelli, Francesco (1702-88)/Private Collection/Photo © Rafael Valls Gallery, London, UK/The Bridgeman Art Library International; page 26: Medea (oil on panel), Sandys, Anthony Frederick Augustus (1829-1904)/© Birmingham Museums and Art Gallery/The Bridgeman Art Library International; page 27: © SuperStock/SuperStock; pages 28, 52: Library of Congress Prints and Photographs Division, Washington, D.C.; page 29: © Bodleian Library, University of Oxford. MS. Douce 167, fol 8r; page 30: © Photo12/The Image Works; page 33: © The Stapleton Collection/Art Resource, NY; page 37: © Ann Ronan Pictures/StockphotoPro; page 38: © The Bridgeman Art Library/SuperStock; page 40: © Harvard Art Museum/Art Resource, NY; page 41: © Laura Bishop/Alamy; pages 43, 46: Erich Lessing/Art Resource, NY; page 49: Ms 3480 Yvain, the Knight with the Lion, fighting a dragon, miniature from Roman de Lancelot (vellum), French School (15th century)/Bibliotheque de L'Arsenal, Paris, France/Archives Charmet/The Bridgeman Art Library International; page 50: akg-images/British Library; page 55: © Grant Faint/Getty Images; page 56: Sea Dragaon (coloured woodcut), Kunisada, Utagawa (1786-1864)/Bibliotheque des Arts Decoratifs, Paris, France/Archives Charmet/The Bridgeman Art Library International.

Printed in the United States of America

Front cover: Saint George, the ideal knight, fights a dragon in a painting by Raphael from the early 1500s.
Half-title page: An illustration of an Ethiopian dragon from a history of dragons published in 1640.
Title page: The archangel Michael attacks the devil in the form of a dragon.
Back cover: A dragonish gargoyle looks down on Paris from high atop Notre Dame Cathedral.

CONTENTS

INTRODUCTION

In the CREATURES OF FANTASY series, we celebrate the deeds of dragons, unicorns, and their kin. These fabulous beasts have inhabited the imagination and arts since the beginnings of human history. They have been immortalized in paintings and sculptures, mythology and literature, movies and video games. Today's blockbuster fantasy novels and films—*The Chronicles of Narnia, Harry Potter, Lord of the Rings, Eragon,* and others—have brought new popularity to the denizens of folklore, myths, and legends. It seems that these creatures of the imagination have always been with us and, in one way or another, always will be.

Belief in the fantastic, in wonders, appears to be a lasting part of the human experience. Even if we no longer believe that dragons and unicorns actually exist, we still like to think about what things might be like if they did. We dream and daydream about them. We make up stories. And as we share those dreams, read and tell those stories, we not only stir our imaginations but also explore some of the deepest hopes and fears of humanity. The power of the dragon, the purity of the unicorn, the wildness of the centaur, the allure of the mermaid—these and more are all part of our human heritage, the legends of our ancestors still alive for us today.

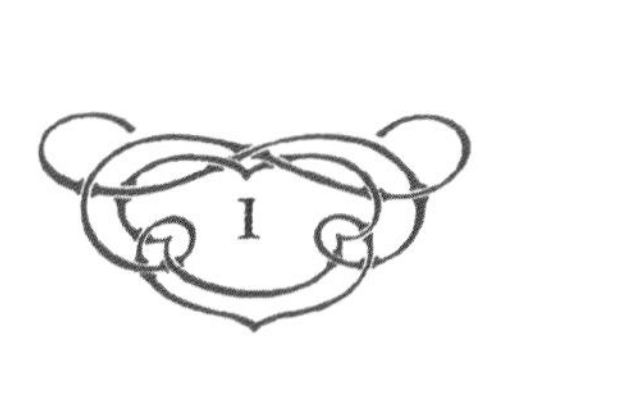

WELCOME TO THE DRAGON'S LAIR

The dragon is the largest of all serpents. Often he is drawn out of his den and rises up into the air, and the air is moved by him and also the sea swells against his venom. Often four or five of them fasten their tails together and rear up their heads and sail over seas and over rivers to get good meat.

~Bartholomew Anglicus, thirteenth century

DRAGONS ARE SNAKELIKE CREATURES. Usually they have wings. Often they breathe fire. They love gold, jewels, and other treasures, which they pile together and guard fiercely. They are famous for terrorizing the countryside and devouring sheep—or, when they can get them, maidens. With habits like these, it's not surprising that where there are dragons, there are usually dragon slayers. Killing dragons has featured on heroes' to-do lists since the very first tales of dragons were written down.

But not all dragons are maiden-eating marauders. Dragons have protected nations and founded empires. They have commanded wind and rain for the benefit of sailors and farmers. They have imparted ancient wisdom to deserving seekers of knowledge. They have

Opposite: Computer art makes a fire-breathing dragon seem almost terrifyingly real.

carried brave riders on their backs. They have symbolized both the fearsome and wondrous aspects of nature and of the imagination.

A Class All Their Own

If dragons could be classified scientifically, they would belong to the reptile class and the family that includes snakes and lizards. Like these animals, dragons are (we assume) cold-blooded—except maybe the ones who breathe fire. They have scales, lay eggs, and do not nurse their young—except occasionally in a fantasy novel where dragon's milk is an important ingredient for magic spells or healing potions. With exceptions like these, it's probably a good thing that scientists don't actually have to classify dragons—who, after all, are really in a class by themselves.

Dragons have been reputed to live in most parts of the world. They thrive in a wide range of habitats, but nearly always live in places where humans seldom go: high, craggy mountains; deep, dark forests; murky, muddy swamps. Many dragons are equally at home on land or in the air. A few are comfortable in the water, but this is mainly the domain of their cousins the sea serpents. These relatives are so close, though, that in some myths and legends it's hard to tell whether the featured creature is a dragon or a sea monster.

Above and opposite: A natural history book published in the 1600s included these illustrations of different types of dragons.

Many species of dragon have been said to exist. As English writer Edward Topsell explained in 1608, "There are diverse sorts of Dragons, distinguished partly by their Countries, partly by their quantity and magnitude [size], partly by the different form of their external parts." Topsell described the diversity of dragons further: "There be some dragons which have wings and no feet, some again have both feet and wings, and some neither feet nor wings, but are only distinguished from the common sort of Serpents by the comb growing upon their heads, and the beard under their cheeks."

Dragons with wings and no feet were sometimes called amphipteres. Closely related to them were the flying serpents that ancient authors said lived in Arabia and India. The Greek historian Herodotus reported several stories about these creatures and pointed out that their wings were featherless, more batlike than birdlike. He even went to a certain place in Arabia to find out for himself about the winged serpents.

> On my arrival I saw the back-bones and ribs of serpents in such numbers as it is impossible to describe. . . . The place where the bones lie is at the entrance of a narrow gorge between steep mountains. . . . The story goes, that with the spring the snakes come flying from Arabia towards Egypt, but are met in this gorge by the birds called ibises, who forbid their entrance and destroy them all.

Dragons with both feet and wings include the classic dragons of European myth and legend. Their wings, like those of the flying serpents, typically resemble a bat's rather than a bird's. Their bodies may be slender and snakelike, or may take a more lizardlike shape, often with a bulky middle in contrast to a long neck and tapering tail. These dragons come in a range of sizes, from gigantic, to the size of two horses, down to the size of a dog. The smallest dragons are often known as dragonets. Dragons with two legs instead of four are frequently called wyverns. While European dragons tend to have long legs like those of most four-footed mammals, dragons of China and Japan have short legs like a lizard's. These Far Eastern dragons often do not have wings, although they can still fly.

Very Big Snakes?

Dragons with neither feet nor wings can be difficult to recognize as dragons—they may just be very, very big snakes. In fact, some languages use the same word for "large serpent" as for "dragon." We can, however, consider many monstrous snakes, especially ones with supernatural powers, to be dragons, or at least their close relatives. Such creatures include the rainbow serpents described in the myths of Aboriginal Australians. These serpents, it is said, sleep deep underground during the dry season. If someone disturbs their rest, they are likely to eat the offender or send a flood to destroy the nearest village. During the rainy season, though, they rise up and shine in the sky with all the colors of the rainbow.

A rainbow serpent decorates a school wall in northern Australia.

Kweku and the Dragon

People tend to think of dragons as creatures of Europe and Asia, yet dragons and their relatives have been known on almost every continent. In a tale from the Ashanti people of West Africa, for instance, the trickster–hero Anansi and his son Kweku Tsin were captured by a fire-breathing dragon. They were thrown into a castle with the dragon's other prisoners, all guarded by a white rooster whose crow would summon the dragon at a moment's notice. But Kweku found forty bags of rice stored in the castle. He ripped them open and scattered the grains everywhere. While the rooster was busy pecking up the tasty rice, Kweku directed the other captives in making a rope ladder. He threw the end of the ladder up to heaven, where the gods caught and held it so that the prisoners could escape. As they began to climb, with Kweku bringing up the rear, the dragon speedily approached. Kweku was ready for him with a bag of cattle bones. He threw the bones to the ground when the dragon drew near, and the hungry monster couldn't resist stopping to gobble them up. When the bones were gone and the dragon advanced again, Kweku played his magic fiddle, which made the dragon stop to dance. As Kweku neared the top of the ladder, the dragon closed in on him once more. Kweku bravely reached down and cut the rope. The dragon crashed to the ground, but the gods grabbed Kweku and pulled him into heaven. There they rewarded him for rescuing the dragon's prisoners by giving him the power of the sun, while his father became the moon and the freed captives became the stars.

Above: Dragonish creatures adorn hand-dyed cloth from West Africa.

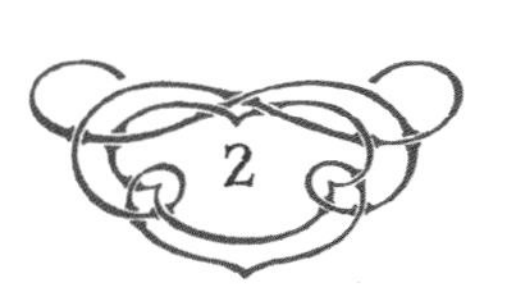

CREATURES FROM THE DAWN OF TIME

She cloaked ferocious dragons with fearsome rays,
And made them bear mantles of radiance, made them godlike. . . .
[She chanted,] "Whoever looks upon them shall collapse in utter terror!"
~*ENUMA ELISH*, SECOND MILLENNIUM BCE

IN THEIR EARLIEST APPEARANCES IN mythology, dragons and their kin were forces of chaos, or disorder. They might cause chaos, or they themselves might be chaos in creature form. Their wild energy was often necessary to get creation going. Sooner or later, though, they generally turned into enemies of the divine order and human civilization.

From ancient Mesopotamia (modern-day Iraq), the *Enuma Elish* is one of humanity's first written myths. It begins with Apsu, god of freshwater, and Tiamat, goddess of salt water and the chaotic depths of the sea. They mingled their waters together and in this way created the elder gods, who then produced still more gods. Eventually the younger gods became so numerous and unruly that Apsu decided to destroy them. Instead, they killed him.

Opposite: The Mesopotamian goddess Tiamat turned herself into a dragon in preparation for battle.

Tiamat, along with the elder gods, swore revenge. To help in the fight, she gave birth to giant snakes, a horned serpent, a dragon called a *mushussu,* and many other monsters. Then she turned herself into a dragon, with horns on her head, two legs, a long slender body, and weaponproof scales on her back. Tiamat and her forces battled the younger gods for some time, with neither side gaining any advantage. Finally, the younger gods' king, Marduk, challenged Tiamat to single combat.

When they came face-to-face in battle, Marduk threw a huge net and entangled Tiamat. Then he let loose a whirlwind that he had created and threw it at her face. She swallowed the whirlwind, and it raged within her and made her swell up so that her belly was stretched and exposed. Marduk shot an arrow into this tender spot, and Tiamat fell dead. He took her body and used half of it to make the sky and half to make the surface of the earth, where Tiamat's waters were contained by the land. Marduk also captured all of her monsters. The *mushussu* dragon not only surrendered to him but became his loyal servant and protector ever afterward.

The Enemy of the Sun

Tiamat has become known as the Mother of Dragons. Most other ancient dragons and chaos serpents, however, were male. In Egypt there was Apep (also called Apophis), who lived in the underworld. This monstrous serpent was the eternal enemy of the sun god Re (or Ra). Every night Re had to sail his boat from the west, where the sun had set, back to the east so that the sun could rise again. And every night Apep tried to devour him, boat and all. In some versions of the myth, Re took the shape of a huge cat and in this form battled and beheaded Apep. In other versions Re

was protected by a guardian serpent or had help from another god or goddess. No matter what, though, Apep would come back to life, ready to attack Re again the next night. And sometimes Apep nearly succeeded in destroying the god, causing an eclipse of the sun. Luckily, Re always escaped the monster's jaws.

The Case of the Stolen Rivers

India's earliest scriptures also tell of a divine dragon slayer: Indra, the sky god. Only he was able to combat the dragon Vitra, enemy of gods and humankind, who had stolen the seven rivers that were the source of all the earth's water. Indra prepared for battle by swallowing three full bowls of the gods' magical strength-giving drink. Then, armed with thunderbolts, he went to the mountaintop where Vitra lay coiled. The dragon breathed out fog so thick that the sky darkened, and sent lightning and hail to attack Indra. But the god was undaunted, and when the lightning flashed he aimed a thunderbolt and hurled it into Vitra's body. The dragon toppled down the mountain, dead. The battle was not yet over, however. Vitra's mother reared up, seeking revenge. Throwing another thunderbolt, Indra killed her, too. Then, with a third thunderbolt, Indra broke open the mountain, where Vitra had hidden away the seven rivers. The waters gushed out, flowing free, and the world was saved from drought and starvation.

A painting on the wall of an ancient Egyptian tomb shows Re as the Great Cat slaying Apep, the serpent of darkness.

A "Fiendish Snake"

Religious texts from ancient Iran told of Azhi Dahaka, a "fiendish snake, three-jawed and triple-headed, six-eyed, of thousand powers and mighty strength, a lie-demon . . . whom the evil spirit Angra Mainyu made." The hero Thraetaona fought, subdued, and imprisoned this terrible dragon. Unfortunately, Azhi Dahaka still had many spies and agents in the world, including the dragon Gandarewa. Gandarewa was a lord of the deepest sea and at one time was keeper of a sacred healing plant, which he sometimes shared with humans. But over time he got greedy, keeping the plant to himself, and he became an enemy of civilization. He met his match, though, in the hero Keresaspa.

Keresaspa had already slain a gigantic dragon named Srvara, "which devoured men and horses, which was venomous and yellow." He'd run along Srvara's back for half a day before finally managing to bring his club down on the monster's neck, killing him with that one blow. Now he faced an even greater challenge, for Gandarewa was cunning as well as huge and fierce. As Keresaspa drew near, the dragon opened his jaws wide, and Keresaspa could see corpses stuck in his teeth. Gandarewa reached out and grabbed the hero's beard, pulled him into the sea, and the fight began. It took nine days for Keresaspa to disable his foe and pull him out of the water.

A "three-jawed and triple-headed, six-eyed" snake uncoils, alert and ready to strike.

Even now Gandarewa was not finished. He promptly killed the fifteen horses that Keresaspa had left waiting on shore, then blinded the hero and kidnapped his family. Keresaspa healed quickly, however, and regained his strength and his sight. He pursued Gandarewa into the sea, rescued his wife and children, and finally succeeded in killing the monster. Because of this success, he was destined to slay the greatest dragon of all, Azhi Dahaka. At the end of time, Azhi Dahaka would escape his prison and menace the world, and Keresaspa would be one of the heroes who would destroy him at last.

Cosmic Serpents and Gods

Some dawn-of-time dragons and serpents were not so much creatures of chaos as of raw power that was neither bad nor good—it just *was.* Such dragons were like any other force of nature: their activities could sometimes harm people, but often were essential for human life. In fact, according to many myths, they were an essential part of the world's creation.

For example, West Africa's cosmic serpent Aido Hwedo carried the god Mawu in his mouth and assisted him in the work of creation. It was Aido Hwedo's dung that piled up to form the earth's mountains. But the earth got so heavy that Mawu decided Aido Hwedo needed to coil up beneath it to support it. This was hot work, so Mawu created the ocean to help cool the giant serpent. Sometimes, though, Aido Hwedo still gets uncomfortable. As he shifts to a better position, he shakes the earth and we have earthquakes.

Aido Hwedo was also known as Da. West Africans who were taken to the Caribbean as slaves brought their tales of Da with them. The great serpent came to be called Damballah, and he is still honored by many people of Haiti today.

Australia's frilled lizard is also known as the dragon lizard. Luckily, it's much smaller than the average dragon of legend.

Where Did Dragons Come From?

It is amazing that so many cultures, in so many parts of the world, have included stories of dragons in their earliest beliefs and writings. Could these dragons have been based on anything real? People have answered this question in various ways over the centuries. Some have explained dragons as exaggerated portraits of real species of snakes and other reptiles. Some have claimed that a few large prehistoric reptiles survived after the dinosaurs' extinction. And some have pointed out that nearly all the places where dragon myths were common were also places where many fossils could be found.

When ancient people came across dinosaur bones, for example, it would have been natural for them to try to figure out what kinds of animals the bones had belonged to. Depending on the types of remains they found, they might explain them as dragons, griffins, or any of several other fantastic creatures. We know that in China in earlier times, nearly all fossils were referred to as "dragon bones." And many ancient Greeks and Romans—including the Roman emperor Augustus—collected fossils, often referring to them as the bones or skeletons of giants and famous monsters. The third-century writer Philostratus, repeating what he had read in the works of a Greek philosopher who traveled in northern India during the first century, said that in the center of one Indian city there were "enshrined a great many skulls of dragons." Sure enough, in the hills and mountains of this region can be found a multitude of fossil remains, including the horned skulls of gigantic giraffelike creatures, looking just as we might imagine dragon skulls.

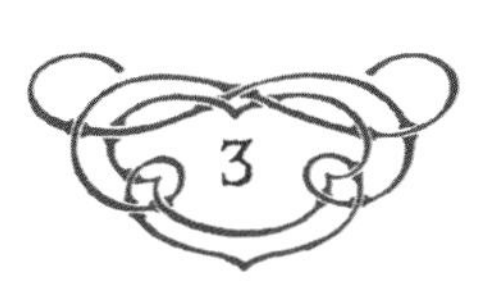

SHARP-EYED SERPENTS

[Various authors] do affirm a Dragon is of a black colour,
the belly somewhat green, and very beautiful to behold,
having . . . most bright and clear-seeing eyes,
which caused the Poets to say in their writings
that these dragons are the watchful keepers of Treasures.

~Edward Topsell, 1608

EUROPE'S OLDEST DRAGON STORIES CAN BE found in the myths and legends of ancient Greece. In fact, our word *dragon* comes from ancient Greek *drakōn.* This word was closely related to the verb meaning "to see, to look at, to watch." And, as with dragons from many other parts of the world, ancient Greek dragons were famous as sharp-sighted guardians who watched over precious things—especially treasures and water sources.

One of the first and most formidable of these dragons was Python, who guarded a spring on Mount Parnassus. Unfortunately, this was where the god Apollo had decided to build his temple, and the great serpent threatened to endanger his worshipers. In

Opposite: Apollo—god of prophecy, healing, and the arts—was the divine dragon slayer of ancient Greece.

the words of the "Hymn to Apollo," from the seventh century BCE, Python was a "bloated, great she-dragon*, a fierce monster wont to do great mischief to men upon earth, to men themselves and to their thin-shanked sheep; for she was a very bloody plague. . . . Whosoever met the dragoness, the day of doom would sweep him away, until the lord Apollo, who deals death from afar, shot a strong arrow at her." That one arrow was enough to kill Python, and Apollo triumphantly built his sanctuary. Python was honored after death, though: the site became known as Pytho, and the priestess who served Apollo there was called the Pythia.

One day a traveler named Cadmus came to Apollo's temple, and the Pythia told him where he should go to found a new city. Cadmus followed her instructions, and soon after reaching the place, he sent his companions to fetch water. The spring they went to, however, was sacred to the war god Ares, and it was guarded by a dragon. This is how the Roman poet Ovid described the creature and his reaction to Cadmus's men:

> His crest was gold,
> His eyes flashed fire, his body swelled with poison;
> Three darting tongues he had, three rows of teeth. . . .
> Twisting his scaly coils in writhing loops,
> Curving in undulant arcs and semicircles,
> The serpent lifts himself erect. . . .
> The whole wood lies beneath him, and he strikes,
> Coils, or constricts, and all the men are victims.

*In the "Hymn to Apollo," Python was female, but in later versions of the story the monster became a male.

When Cadmus went looking for his companions, he found them dead, with the dragon licking their wounds. Cadmus hurled a boulder at the monster, who remained uninjured. Next Cadmus threw his javelin, and the iron point lodged in the dragon's spine. He was finally finished off by Cadmus's spear. Then Athena, the goddess of wisdom, appeared and told Cadmus to take the dragon's teeth and plant them in the ground. Cadmus did so, and immediately a troop of fully armed warriors grew from these strange seeds. The instant they emerged, the men began to fight one another, till only five were left alive. The survivors became Cadmus's steadfast friends and advisers and helped him establish his new city.

In a painting from the 1700s, Cadmus slays the dragon who killed his followers.

Medea and the Dragons

Warriors grown from dragon teeth were a problem for another Greek hero, Jason. He had come to Colchis, on the eastern shore of the Black Sea, to get the Golden Fleece. This was the wool of a divine ram, which Jason believed would lift a curse from his homeland. But the king of Colchis demanded that Jason first harness two ferocious bulls and make them pull a plow, then plant a

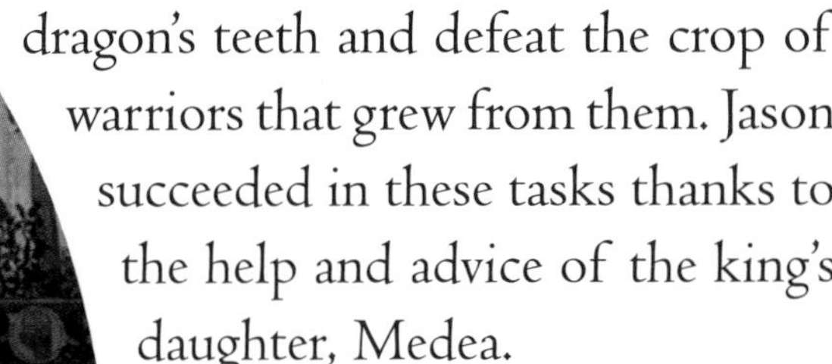

dragon's teeth and defeat the crop of warriors that grew from them. Jason succeeded in these tasks thanks to the help and advice of the king's daughter, Medea.

Medea was both intelligent and skilled in magic, and she went with Jason to the place where the Golden Fleece hung in a tree. The fleece was guarded by a huge dragon with, as one ancient writer put it, "keen sleepless eyes." Medea lulled the dragon by singing magical chants so that she could get close enough to sprinkle it with a sleeping potion. While it dozed, Jason pulled the Golden Fleece out of the tree. Then he slew the monster—although in some versions of the legend, the dragon was killed by Medea. The couple returned to Greece with their treasure and were married. Eventually, however, Jason betrayed Medea. After taking her revenge, she climbed into a chariot pulled by two winged dragons, and was never heard from again.

Medea, portrayed by a nineteenth-century artist, prepares one of her magical potions.

Heracles and the Hydra

One of Jason's companions on the journey to Colchis was Heracles (also known as Hercules), a hero who did battle with more than one dragonish foe. Among these creatures was the Hydra, whose father was a monster named Typhon. The early Greek poet Hesiod wrote that Typhon had a hundred dragon heads, and "from all his heads fire burned as he glared. And in all his terrible heads were voices that uttered all manner of cries unspeakable." It had taken the king of the gods, Zeus himself, to defeat Typhon and imprison him beneath a volcano. Now it was up to Zeus's half-human son Heracles to vanquish the Hydra.

The Hydra lived in a swamp. Like its father, it had numerous heads—nine in some versions of the story, as many as a hundred or even a thousand in others. Every head was a hissing poisonous serpent, and one of the heads was immortal. The others had an uncanny power: when one was chopped off, two more would grow in its place. Even for a hero as great as Heracles, it was nearly impossible to defeat this creature. He finally succeeded, though, with the help of his friend Iolaus. Immediately after Heracles chopped off each of the monster's heads, Iolaus used a torch to burn the neck so that it couldn't sprout new heads. Heracles at last cut off the immortal head and buried it beneath the heaviest rock around. The Hydra was a menace no longer.

Heracles confronts the Hydra in its swampy lair in an 1867 painting by Gustave Moreau.

Later, Heracles was sent on a quest for the golden apples of the Hesperides. The Hesperides were daughters of the Evening Star, and the apples that grew on the tree in their garden could grant eternal youth. Naturally, these precious treasures had to be

protected. This was the job of a dragon named Ladon, another of Typhon's ferocious brood.* But fierce though Ladon was, he was no match for Heracles, who killed him and took the golden apples.

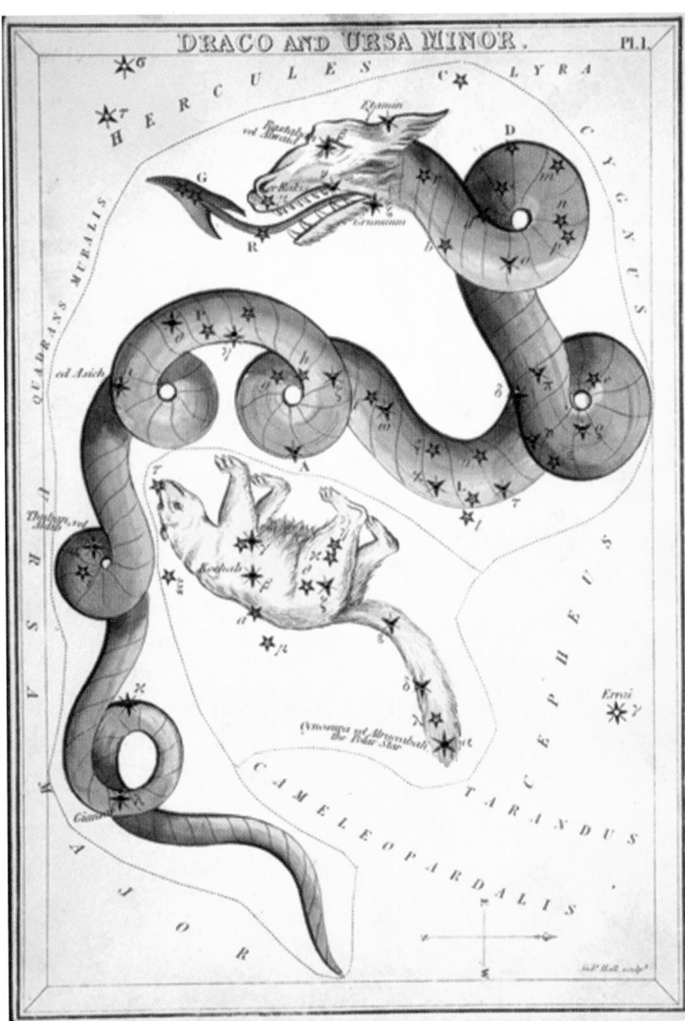

Draco curls around Ursa Minor (also known as the Little Dipper) in an imaginative 1825 illustration of the constellations.

Heracles was so proud of this feat that he had his shield decorated with the dragon's image, as described by Hesiod: "On [the shield's] centre was the unspeakable terror of a dragon glancing backward with eyes gleaming with fire. His mouth, too, was filled with teeth running in a white line, dread and unapproachable." The queen of the gods, Hera, commemorated Ladon in another way: she turned his body into the constellation Draco "the dragon."

*The mother of Ladon and the Hydra, along with several other monsters, was Echidna, a beautiful woman from the waist up and a snake from the waist down.

The Basilisk

This relative of the dragon was known as the king of serpents—its name comes from a Greek word for "king," *basileus*. The classic description of the basilisk is by first-century Roman author Pliny the Elder.

> It is deadly to the human race, as all who see its eyes expire immediately. The basilisk serpent . . . is a native of the province of Cyrenaica [eastern Libya], not more than 12 inches long, and adorned with a bright white marking on the head like a sort of diadem [crown]. It routs all snakes with its hiss, and does not move its body forward in manifold coils like the other snakes but advancing with its middle raised high. It kills bushes not only by its touch but also by its breath, scorches up grass and bursts rocks. Its effect on other animals is disastrous; it is believed that once one was killed with a spear by a man on horseback and the infection rising through the spear killed not only the rider but also the horse. Yet to a creature so marvellous as this . . . the venom of weasels is fatal: so fixed is the decree of nature that nothing shall be without its match. They throw the basilisks into weasels' holes, which are easily known by the foulness of the ground, and the weasels kill them by their stench.

Above: A birdlike basilisk fights its mortal enemy, the weasel.

MONSTERS OF THE NORTH

Come not between the Dragon and his wrath.

~WILLIAM SHAKESPEARE, SIXTEENTH CENTURY

NORTHERN EUROPE HAS BEEN HOME TO much dragon lore, along with a number of different words for this fantastic creature. Greek *drakōn* and Latin *draco* became German *Drache,* Norse *dreki,* Welsh *draig,* and English *dragon* and *drake.* Other words meaning "dragon" include Old English *wyrm,* German *wurm,* and Norse *ormr.* Such words often turn up in the names of places that were associated with dragons, for example Wormley and Drakelow in England, and Drachenfels and Worms in Germany. Dragons, it appears, were a fairly normal part of the northern landscape.

Like the dragons of Greece, northern dragons were well known for guarding valuables. An Old English proverb said, "The dragon shall [be] on the barrow, proud, arrogant in treasures." A barrow was an ancient burial mound. Such mounds, along with caves, were

Opposite: The German hero Siegfried slays a dragon by striking at its vulnerable underside.

especially appealing to dragons. The creatures might lie hidden for centuries in these dark places, contented amid their riches—until something, or someone, disturbed them.

Beowulf's Tragic End

The Old English epic poem *Beowulf* illustrated the dangers of disturbing a dragon. Written down around 1000 but probably taking place in the 500s, the poem told the story of Beowulf, a renowned warrior from what is now Sweden. In the second half of the poem, Beowulf had become king and had ruled his country in peace and plenty for fifty years. But the peace was shattered when one of his subjects stole a golden cup from a sleeping dragon's hoard. The dragon awoke, enraged by the theft.

> Then the baleful stranger belched fire and flame,
> Burned the bright dwellings—the glow of the blaze
> Filled hearts with horror. The hostile flier
> Was minded to leave there nothing alive.

Beowulf prepared his weapons and armor and tracked the dragon to its lair. In his first attack his sword thrust failed to cut deeply enough to wound the monster. It struck back by breathing fire at the hero. Beowulf renewed his assault; the dragon grew fiercer. One of Beowulf's companions, a young man named Wiglaf, rushed to help him. The dragon immediately burned Wiglaf's shield to ashes. Protecting Wiglaf with his own shield, Beowulf once again swung his sword; this time it broke against his foe's head.

The monster seized Beowulf by the throat. Wiglaf darted forward, plunging his sword in just below the dragon's head. It released Beowulf, who drew his dagger "and slit asunder the worm with the blow." But the dragon's venom had already begun to work in the hero's wounds. Soon Beowulf was dead. His people threw the dragon's body into the sea and buried its hoarded jewels and gold with their beloved king. So ended the greatest dragon fight in English literature.

Beowulf lies dying beside the dragon he killed to save his people.

Awful Warnings and Dire Signs

For the early English people, dragons were not just the villains in exciting stories. They were also monsters in the original sense of the word, which comes from Latin *monstrum,* "an omen"—a sign or warning. For example, *The Anglo-Saxon Chronicle,* compiled between 890 and 1154, recorded that the year 793 "began with ominous signs over Northumbria [northern England], and these utterly panicked the people. Huge streaks of flame rushed across the full length of the sky, and flaming dragons as well were seen

flying through the air." People believed these sights warned that something awful was going to happen. In June 793 the Vikings made their first recorded raid on England. These northern pirates would continue to harass England (and many other countries) for almost three centuries.

The Vikings are also referred to as the Norse, especially when we're talking about the people who did not go out raiding. Their homeland was the region known as Scandinavia—modern Norway, Denmark, and Sweden—and they also settled Iceland and Greenland. These rugged lands seem to have offered plenty of inspiration for stories of fantastic creatures: more than three dozen dragons inhabit Norse literature and legends.

The most famous of all Norse dragons was named Fafnir. But Fafnir did not start off as a dragon; he was once a man. When one of his brothers was killed, his father accepted a large amount of gold in compensation. The gold, however, carried a curse that would destroy whoever owned it. Sure enough, soon Fafnir and his surviving brother, Regin, murdered their father because he would not share the gold with them. Then Fafnir took all the gold for himself, threatening to kill Regin. Regin fled and, in the words of the thirteenth-century Icelandic writer Snorri Sturluson, "Fafnir went up on to Gnita Heath and, making a lair there, turned himself into a dragon and lay down on the gold."

Regin settled in another country, where he worked as a smith, plotted to get the gold for himself, and raised a boy named Sigurd as his foster son. When Sigurd came of age, Regin forged a marvelous sword for him and encouraged him to try it out on the horrible dragon Fafnir. Sigurd agreed, and the two set out for Gnita Heath. Once there, Sigurd dug pits in the ground, right in the path leading to Fafnir's lair. He concealed himself in one of the holes, sword at the ready. As Snorri told it, "When Fafnir, crawling on his way down to the water, came over the pit, Sigurd ran him through with his sword and that was his death. Then Regin came and said that Sigurd had killed his brother, and offered him terms on condition that he took Fafnir's heart and roasted it over a fire."

Sigurd set about roasting the heart. When he poked it to see if it was done, hot juices burst out and burned his finger. He quickly put the finger in his mouth—and the second he tasted this bit of dragon's heart, he could understand the language of the birds. From the birds in a nearby tree, he learned that Regin planned to murder him. He turned around and killed Regin first. Then he went to Fafnir's lair, took all of the dragon's gold, and rode away with it to further adventures.*

Merlin and the Dragons

Another famous dragon legend comes from Wales, the western country that shares the island of Great Britain with England and Scotland. The story was recorded around 1136 by a scholar named Geoffrey of Monmouth. He told how Vortigern, king of the Britons, had hired Saxon warriors (from what is now northern Germany) to fight against his enemies. The Saxons got out of hand and began to take over, so Vortigern ordered the building of a tower where he could go for safety. The masons made no progress, however, because at the end of every day the earth swallowed up whatever they had built. Vortigern's magicians told him the tower's foundations would only hold firm if he killed a certain boy and

*There are several tellings of this story from northern Europe; in German versions the hero is called Siegfried.

Amazed, King Vortigern watches the fight between the red and white dragons, as imagined by an artist in the 1400s.

sprinkled his blood on the building stones. That boy was Merlin, who was destined to become a far greater magician than those who advised the king.

When Merlin was brought to Vortigern, he revealed the real problem with the tower: beneath the earth in that spot was a pool, within which two dragons lay sleeping. This turned out to be true. And as the amazed king stood by the pool after the water was drained, the dragons awoke and flew out.

> As soon as they were near enough to each other, they fought bitterly, breathing out fire as they panted. The White Dragon began to have the upper hand and to force the Red One back to the edge of the pool. The Red Dragon bewailed the fact that it was being driven out and then turned upon the White One and forced it backwards in its turn.

Merlin explained that the White Dragon represented the Saxons, while the Red Dragon stood for the Britons, the native people of Britain. Indeed, for centuries the Red Dragon has been the proud symbol of Wales, home to many of the descendants of the ancient Britons.

The Sign of the Dragon

One of the rulers who came after Vortigern was named Uther. Before he became king, according to Geoffrey of Monmouth, a huge, bright star appeared, "with a single beam shining from it. At the end of this beam was a ball of fire, spread out in the shape of a dragon." Merlin told Uther this was a sign that he would be the next king, that his son would be a great king after him, and that his daughter's sons and grandsons would also rule. Uther then had a golden dragon made as his battle standard, and from that time on he had the added name Pendragon, which in the language of the Britons meant "a dragon's head." Uther's son was King Arthur, and he continued to use the dragon as his symbol. For this fabled royal family, the dragon was a powerful guardian.

In northern Europe, it seems, dragons could often be allies. In some circumstances, the dragon granted protection, strength, and good fortune—or at least its image did. All kinds of objects from Britain and Scandinavia were decorated with dragons, including jewelry as well as weapons and shields. In Scandinavia carvings of dragons even adorned some churches. Perhaps the most famous Scandinavian guardian dragons were the wooden beasts used as figureheads on Viking ships. These served the dual purpose of protecting the crew and striking fear into the people they attacked. When Vikings sailed into a friendly port, they showed their peaceful intentions by removing the fearsome figureheads.

Above: A fanciful but fearsome dragon-prowed Viking ship, from a tenth-century English manuscript.

5

ENEMIES OF GOD

And then there was war in heaven. . . .
And the great dragon was cast out,
that old serpent, called the Devil, and Satan,
which deceiveth the whole world.
~REVELATION 12:7–9

IN THE BIBLICAL STORY OF THE GARDEN OF Eden, a serpent tempted Eve, the first woman, to eat the forbidden fruit of knowledge. This serpent was identified with Satan, and in art it was often portrayed as a devilish winged dragon. In Christian scripture and legend, dragons became almost completely evil, the enemies of God and the church, foes of all that was holy.

Revelation, the last book of the Bible, described Satan in the form of "a great red dragon, having seven heads and ten horns, and seven crowns upon his heads." The archangel Michael fought and defeated this dragon, and cast him out of heaven and onto the earth. Here the dragon made war against humankind. Toward the end of time, the angel and the dragon would resume their battle.

Opposite: The warrior-angel Michael battles the forces of hell in a painting by the great Italian artist Raphael.

The author of Revelation had a vision that foretold this event: "I saw an angel come down from heaven, having the key of the bottomless pit and a great chain in his hand. And he laid hold on the dragon, . . . and bound him a thousand years, and cast him into the bottomless pit, and shut him up, and set a seal upon him, that he should deceive the nations no more." When the thousand years were up, the biblical account continued, Satan would briefly break free but would then be thrown into "the lake of fire and brimstone . . . for ever and ever."

Poet and artist William Blake painted this 1805 watercolor of Michael chaining up the dragon and preparing to throw him into the bottomless pit.

Given these scriptures, many early Christians naturally thought of dragons as allies of the devil. So it is not surprising that a number of Christian saints, or holy people, were dragon fighters. Sometimes this didn't work out so well for them. For example, Saint Philip, who had been one of Jesus's twelve disciples, drove out a dragon that lived in a temple in what is now Turkey. As the dragon left, however, it spewed poison on the watching crowd, injuring and killing many. The townspeople blamed Saint Philip for this calamity, and he ended up being executed.

Other saints were more successful in their encounters with dragons. Saint Guthmund overcame one by praying and sprinkling it with holy water. All it took for Saint Donatus to kill a dragon was to spit in its mouth. Saint Marcel defeated a dragon that was threatening Paris by hitting it on the head with a cross. Then he escorted it out of town, made it promise to stay in the woods, and set it free. Saint Samson in Wales and Saint Germanus in Scotland both bravely marched into dragons' dens and led the beasts out. Samson flung his dragon into the sea, while Germanus threw his into a pit.

One of the many gargoyles on Notre Dame Cathedral in Paris.

In the year 520, according to legend, a dragon called the Gargouille went on a rampage in the countryside around Rouen, in northern France. Not only did it eat anyone it could catch, but it also spouted huge fountains of water that swamped farmers' fields and sank boats on the Seine River. The bishop of Rouen, Saint Romain, decided he had to save his people. The only person who would help him was a prisoner who had been condemned to death. As soon as the bishop and the prisoner got to the Gargouille's cave, the monster charged them and prepared to unleash a flood of water. But Saint Romain held up his hands with his index fingers forming a cross. This holy sign completely subdued the Gargouille, allowing the prisoner to bind it and take it back to town. There it was put to death, while the brave prisoner was pardoned and set free. To this day, waterspouts on French churches are called gargoyles after the Gargouille.

Saint Martha and Saint Margaret

Like Saint Romain, Saint Martha used an improvised cross to defeat a dragonish foe. During the days of the Roman Empire, a monster called the Tarasque was terrorizing an area in southern France. Sixteen men tried to destroy it, but half of them were killed by one fiery blast from the Tarasque's mouth. Then Saint Martha arrived on the scene. When she heard about the Tarasque, she promised to put an end to its murderous ways. She went into the woods and almost immediately came upon the monster. As it turned its burning eyes toward her, she seized two branches from the ground and held them up in the shape of a cross. The Tarasque lay down at her feet, allowing her to sprinkle it with holy water and leash it with her own braided hair. Saint Martha took the beast into the nearest town to show the people that it was reformed—but their desire for revenge was too great, and they killed it.

Another female saint who faced a dragon was Saint Margaret of Antioch. She had been imprisoned for refusing to marry a Roman official who was not a Christian. While she sat praying in her cell, a dragon appeared and attacked her. In one version of the legend, she made the sign of the cross, and the creature simply disappeared. In another version the dragon swallowed her whole. Then, inside its

Raphael's 1520 painting of Saint Margaret, who escaped from a dragon through the power of the cross.

belly, she made the sign of the cross. This caused the dragon to burst open, and she emerged unharmed.

Saint Margaret was a very popular saint during the Middle Ages (roughly 500–1500). Her tale was told in one of medieval Europe's best-loved books, *The Golden Legend*. This thirteenth-century work also contained the story of the most famous dragon-slaying saint of all, Saint George. According to *The Golden Legend*, Saint George was a Christian knight from what is now Turkey, then part of the Roman Empire. His adventure with the dragon, however, occurred in North Africa, outside a city called Silene.

The Lottery

In a swamp or lake near Silene, there lived a dragon whose foul breath poisoned the air of the countryside, and when he came near the city "he venomed the people with his breath." To keep the dragon from doing further harm, the people started feeding him two sheep a day. When they ran out of sheep, they passed a law requiring all the young people of the town to put their names in a lottery. Each week a name was drawn, and that girl or boy was delivered to the dragon—until one day this lot fell to the king's own daughter. The sorrowing king had her dress in her wedding clothes, since she would never get to be a bride. He gave her his blessing and left her weeping beside the dragon's watery lair.

The grateful princess looks on as Saint George defeats the dragon who was going to eat her.

Soon Saint George came riding along and asked the princess what was the matter. She told him, and tried to persuade him to go away so that the dragon would not kill him, too. Even as they were speaking, the dragon emerged from the water. The saintly knight immediately drew his sword, made the sign of the cross, and "rode hardily against the dragon which came toward him, and smote him with his spear and hurt him sore." Then he instructed the princess to tie her sash around the dragon's neck. Together they led the dragon into Silene. Once they reached the city center, Saint George addressed the people, telling them that if they would all become Christians, he would kill the monster. So "the king was baptized and all his people, and Saint George slew the dragon and smote off his head." Then, having given the king some advice about churches and charity, Saint George rode off to rid the world of other evils.

A Dragonish God

While many religious traditions portrayed dragons as agents of evil, the mythology of Mexico and Central America featured a dragonish being as the good guy, the hero who *fought* evil. This deity was the Feathered Serpent, known as Kukulkan to the Mayas and Quetzalcoatl to the Toltecs and Aztecs. It was said that Quetzalcoatl created the human beings currently on the earth by gathering up the broken bones of humans who had been wiped out during the previous age. Quetzalcoatl ground these remains and added some blood from the gods, and from this mixture he formed the new humans. Then he taught them how to grow corn, weave cloth, polish jade, observe the stars, and other useful skills. But the humans and Quetzalcoatl both had a great enemy, Tezcatlipoca, god of darkness and deception. Quetzalcoatl fought this god constantly but, according to one myth, Tezcatlipoca eventually gained the upper hand and succeeded in destroying all the Toltecs. Despairing because he had failed to save his people, Quetzalcoatl set off on a journey through the mountains. His enemy pursued him and robbed him of nearly all his powers and possessions. When Quetzalcoatl reached the sea, he made a raft out of snakes and sailed away. The Aztecs foretold, however, that one day the Feathered Serpent would return to them, restored to his full might and glory.

Above: Winged or feathered serpents are part of dragon lore around the world.

tristan

6

QUESTING BEASTS

Then Sir Lancelot drew his sword and fought with that dragon long, and at last with great pain Sir Lancelot slew that dragon.

~SIR THOMAS MALORY, FIFTEENTH CENTURY

THE SAINT GEORGE LEGEND SET A PATTERN for many of the heroes of medieval literature. For these knights, dragon slaying was almost a requirement, the ultimate proof of their courage and selflessness. It was part of their job to go on quests, adventures that would help their king or their soul or the common good, or all of the above. What better quest could there be than to hunt down a ferocious dragon that was threatening the countryside?

The Questing Beast was perhaps not exactly a dragon, but it certainly was a related species. It had the head of a snake, a leopard's body, a lion's hindquarters, and feet like a deer. The great King Arthur himself encountered it near a spring while hunting in the

Opposite: Sir Tristram, one of King Arthur's knights, killed a dragon that was terrorizing Ireland.

forest, as related by fifteenth-century English writer Sir Thomas Malory: "He thought he heard a noise of hounds, to the sum of thirty. And with that the king saw coming toward him the strangest beast that ever he saw or heard of; so the beast went to the well and drank, and the noise was in the beast's belly."

Shortly after the creature went on its way, the knight Sir Pellenore arrived in pursuit of it. Pellenore explained that he had a destiny to hunt the Questing Beast—but he never did manage to catch it. The creature was finally killed by another knight, Sir Palamedes.

Sir Palamedes was only one of the famous knights of King Arthur's court. Two of the greatest were Sir Gawain and Sir Lancelot, who performed many deeds of valor and battled dragons with great success. Other knights had interesting dragonish experiences as well.

The Knight and the Lion

One of Arthur's knights rescued an unusual victim from a dragon. It happened this way: While riding through a forest, Sir Yvain heard a high, sorrowful cry. Following it to its source, he discovered a lion whose tail was gripped in the jaws of a terrible venomous serpent. The serpent's mouth shot out jets of fire that burned the lion's haunches. Yvain immediately took pity and called out to the lion to hold fast. Yet the knight hesitated. If he killed the dragon, the lion might then turn on him. But Yvain decided it was his duty to help the noble beast, whatever happened afterward. He drew his sword, charged, and easily cut the villainous serpent in two. The head, however, still gripped the lion's tail. Carefully, Yvain freed the lion from the dragon's jaws. The lion then bowed down to him in humble gratitude, and was his loyal and helpful companion ever afterward.

Yvain became known as the Knight of the Lion after he rescued the noble beast from a dragon.

Twelve Heads Are Worse Than One

Russian legends told of a brave knight named Dobrynya Nikitich and his battles with Goryshche, a twelve-headed dragon who hunted young humans to feed to her many children. Nikitich first killed a number of the baby dragons, arousing Goryshche's fury. She chased after him until he found a magical hat that gave him power over dragons. With its help, he was able to chop off eleven of Goryshche's heads. She pleaded with him not to cut off her last head and promised she wouldn't harm any more of the Russian people. But no sooner had Nikitich left the scene than Goryshche kidnapped a princess, whose royal uncle sent Nikitich back out to finish off the dragon. The knight tracked Goryshche to her lair, killed her entire brood of young dragons, and then battled her for three days. At last he was victorious. He released all the humans Goryshche had imprisoned in her den and took the princess back to the capital city, where he was welcomed as a hero.

Dragon Slayers of Persia

Europe was not the only home of dragon-slaying warriors. In his celebrated epic *Shahnameh,* completed around 1010, the Persian poet Firdawi recounted many stories of his country's kings and heroes. Among the greatest of these heroes was the legendary Rustam. One night on a journey, Rustam stopped to rest, not realizing that his campsite was close to a dragon's den. While he slept, the dragon came out. It was "eighty yards in length, and so fierce that neither elephant nor demon nor lion ever ventured to pass by its lair." As the dragon drew near the sleeping hero, Rustam's faithful horse, Rakhsh, neighed and kicked and stamped to awaken him. But just as Rustam woke up, the dragon vanished. After the hero fell back asleep, the same thing happened again. The third time the dragon approached, however, Rakhsh succeeded in waking Rustam before the beast could disappear. Together horse and hero fought the monster, with Rakhsh biting and tearing at the dragon's hide until Rustam got the opening he needed to cut off the dragon's head.

A Persian painting from around 1640 shows Rakhsh biting the dragon while Rustam climbs onto its back to give it the deathblow.

Shahnameh also celebrated the deeds of King Gushtasp and his son Isfendiyar, both of whom were dragon slayers. While Gushtasp attacked his dragon with arrows, spear, and dagger, Isfendiyar approached his quest in an unusual way. He had heard in advance about his reptilian foe.

Fire sparkles round him; his stupendous bulk
Looks like a mountain. When incensed his roar
Makes the surrounding country shake with fear.
White poison foam drips from his hideous jaws,
Which, yawning wide, display a dismal gulf,
The grave of many a hapless being.

Knowing all this, Isfendiyar ordered the building of a special armored chariot. It had an enclosed box for him to sit in and sharp swords sticking out all around the outside. When it was ready, he climbed in, and two horses pulled the chariot to where the dragon waited.

When the dragon heard the rumble of the approaching vehicle, it sped toward Isfendiyar, bellowing with rage. The hero prayed to God for help, even as the dragon opened its huge mouth and swallowed the horses and chariot. But they got stuck in the monster's throat, which was pierced and cut by the swords on the outside of the vehicle. While the dragon was choking and bleeding, Isfendiyar climbed out of the chariot box and plunged his sword into the creature's brain. Then the warrior fainted, overcome by the poisonous fumes from the dragon's venom. When he came to, the dragon lay dead. Isfendiyar gave thanks to God for his victory, and went on to have many more adventures.

Hasegawa
Tokyo Japan

DRAGONS OF THE EAST

The dragon is the chief of scaly reptiles:
in the spring he mounts the heavens,
in the autumn he frequents the streams.
This is favourable.

~A Chinese encyclopedia, 1718

WE HAVE ALREADY MET SOME ASIAN dragons, slain by gods and heroes of Mesopotamia, India, and Persia. But other dragons and dragonlike beings of the East were very different in nature from those monsters. In China, dragons were symbols of divine power and protection for the country's rulers. The five-clawed imperial dragon decorated the emperor's clothes, his palace, his banners, and so on. It was a crime punishable by death for anyone else to use this image. All other dragons had to be depicted with four claws on each foot.

Opposite: Stirring up the waves, a dragon rises out of the sea below Mount Fuji in Japan.

For thousands of years the dragon has played a major role in the beliefs and legends of China. One early myth told of Nu Gua, a goddess with the tail of a dragon. She used yellow mud to

create the first people, then taught them to marry and have children. Eventually she herself married her dragon-tailed brother, Fu Hsi, who taught the people to hunt, fish, write, and make music. In gratitude they made him the first emperor. The emperor who came after Fu Hsi was the son of a dragon. Next on the throne was the fabled Yellow Emperor, who ended his prosperous hundred-year reign by flying to heaven on a dragon's back.

Dragon Details

Chinese dragons were traditionally classified into four main types. The *t'ien lung,* or celestial dragon, was the protector of heaven and guardian of the gods. The *shen lung* was the spiritual dragon, who lived in the sky and controlled clouds and rain. The *ti'lung* lived on the earth and had dominion over rivers and streams. The *fu-ts'ang lung* was the treasure dragon, dwelling deep within the earth where gems and precious metals were found.

Chinese scholars and philosophers described the characteristics of dragons in great detail. For example, a book from the 1500s said that the dragon was a combination of many other animals. Its head was like a camel's, its eyes like a hare's or demon's. It had a cow's ears, a deer's antlers, a snake's neck, and a clam's belly. Its scales were like a fish's, and it had tiger feet with eagle claws. "Its voice resembles the beating of a gong. On each side of its mouth are whiskers, under its chin is a bright pearl. . . . When its breath escapes it forms clouds, sometimes changing into rain, at other times into fire."

Other writings explained the dragon's life cycle. Dragon mothers laid gemlike eggs that took a thousand years to hatch. A newborn dragon was similar to a water snake, and it took five hundred

An imperial dragon on a wall in Beijing's Forbidden City palace, once the home of China's emperors.

years to reach its next stage of development, when its head came to resemble that of a fish. Over the next thousand years, its skin transformed to fish scales, while its body grew long and slender, with four short legs and clawed feet. At the same time its head elongated and sprouted a beard. Over the next five hundred years, it grew a pair of horns. It took another thousand years for its wings to develop, and at this point the dragon was at last fully mature—and completely magnificent.

It wasn't only while they were growing that dragons changed their appearance. It was well known that they were shape-shifters, who could take the forms of various animals and even of humans. One writer described their fluid, mutable qualities this way:

> The dragon's skin has five colours, and he moves like a spirit; he wishes to be small and he becomes like a silkworm; great, and he fills all below heaven; he desires to rise, and he reaches the ether; he desires to sink, and he enters the deep fountains. The times of his changing are not fixed, his rising and descending are undetermined; he is called a god.

Dragons in Japan

Japanese dragons were much like those of China. The main differences in appearance were that they had spines down their backs and only three claws on each foot. A nineteenth-century author writing about Japanese beliefs described several different types of dragons. One kind had incredibly keen vision; another specialized in hoarding treasures. There were water dragons who created rain, and fire dragons who were "only seven feet long." One sort of dragon was nine different colors, while others were just one: green, red, yellow, black, white, or purple. White dragons breathed into the earth, and their breath turned into gold. Similarly, the spit of purple dragons turned into precious crystal spheres.

An 1860 print by the famous Japanese artist Kunisada shows a sea dragon carrying a group of sages over the water.

In Japanese lore there were only a few dragons who posed a direct threat to humans. Of course, water dragons' weather-related activities could sometimes have bad effects for people, if there was too much snow or rain, or too little. There was also a dragon sea god who sometimes caused problems. He had two magical pearls that controlled the ebb and flow of the tides. If these got out of hand, the sea might recede too far, or the waves might rush in and flood the land. Fortunately, in times of flood or drought, Japan's priests had prayers and ceremonies that could convince the dragons to put things back in balance. Dragons listened to the appeals of ordinary people, too—in general, they wanted to be helpful to humanity.

Transformations

Sometimes dragons transformed themselves into humans—and occasionally, a person might be changed into a dragon. This happened to a Buddhist priest named Genko, who decided that he would be able to master all of the Buddha's teachings only if he had a dragon's long life span, which was many thousands of years. So Genko held a drop of water in his hand and meditated until rain clouds formed around him. Then he rose up on the clouds and flew to a pond, where he continued to meditate until he died. Instantly, he was reborn as a dragon. He lived at the pond thereafter, and twice a year received offerings of rice from the local people and granted their wishes.

Japan—and indeed, most of the world—is full of many other marvelous and well-loved dragon stories. In 1904 the Japanese author Kakuzo Okakura summed up the magical essence of the dragon:

> He is the spirit of change, therefore of life itself. . . . Hidden in the caverns of inaccessible mountains, or coiled in the unfathomed depths of the sea, he awaits the time when he slowly arouses himself into activity. He unfolds himself in the storm-clouds; he washes his mane in the darkness of the seething whirlpools. His claws are in the fork of the lightning, his scales begin to glisten in the bark of rain-swept pine-trees. His voice is heard in the hurricane. . . . The dragon reveals himself only to vanish.

No wonder this fantastic creature continues to fascinate us.

Glossary

Aboriginal Refers to the first, or original, people of Australia.

chaos serpent A snakelike or dragonish being who embodies or symbolizes disorder.

epic A long poem about the adventures of one or more legendary heroes.

hoard A collection of treasures, often piled together and hidden away.

mason Someone skilled at stonecutting or building with stone.

myth A traditional story about divine and semidivine beings; myths help people explain life's mysteries.

scriptures Religious writings; holy books.

smith Someone who makes metal tools or weapons.

trickster-hero A hero who usually succeeds through cleverness and trickery rather than by fighting.

To Learn More about Dragons

Books

Allen, Judy. *Fantasy Encyclopedia*. Boston: Kingfisher, 2005.

Baynes, Pauline. *Questionable Creatures: A Bestiary*. Grand Rapids, MI: William B. Eerdmans Publishing Company, 2006.

Mayo, Margaret. *Mythical Birds and Beasts from Many Lands*. New York: Dutton Children's Books, 1996.

McCaffrey, Anne, with Richard Woods. *A Diversity of Dragons*. New York: HarperPrism, 1997.

Mortensen, Lori. *Basilisks*. Farmington Hills, MI: KidHaven Press, 2006.

Nigg, Joseph. *The Book of Dragons and Other Mythical Beasts*. Hauppauge, NY: Barron's, 2002.

Websites

American Museum of Natural History. *Mythic Creatures*. www.amnh.org/exhibitions/past-exhibitions-mythic-creatures

Atsma, Aaron J. *Theoi Greek Mythology: Dragons*.

www.theoi.com/greek-mythology/dragons.html

McCormick, Kylie. *The Circle of the Dragon.* www.blackdrago.com/index.html

Scott, Michon. *Dinosaurs and Dragons.* www.strangescience.net/stdino2.htm

Selected Bibliography

Allan, Tony. *The Mythic Bestiary: The Illustrated Guide to the World's Most Fantastical Creatures.* London: Duncan Baird, 2008.

Bonfante-Warren, Alexandra. *Mythical Beasts: Traditions and Tales of Favorite Fabled Creatures.* New York: MetroBooks, 2000.

Cherry, John, ed. *Mythical Beasts.* San Francisco: Pomegranate Artbooks, 1995.

Delacampagne, Ariane, and Christian Delacampagne. *Here Be Dragons: A Fantastic Bestiary*. Princeton, NJ: Princeton University Press, 2003.

Dobell, Steve. *Dragons: Heroes and Legendary Beasts in Poems, Prose and Paintings.* London: Southwater, 2004.

Gould, Charles. *Dragons, Unicorns, and Sea Serpents: A Classic Study of the Evidence for Their Existence.* 1886. Reprint, Mineola, NY: Dover, 2002.

Ingersoll, Ernest. *Dragons and Dragon Lore.* 1928. Reprint, Mineola, NY: Dover, 2005.

Mayor, Adrienne. *The First Fossil Hunters: Paleontology in Greek and Roman Times.* Princeton, NJ: Princeton University Press, 2000.

Nigg, Joseph. *The Book of Fabulous Beasts: A Treasury of Writings from Ancient Times to the Present.* New York: Oxford University Press, 1999.

———. *Wonder Beasts: Tales and Lore of the Phoenix, the Griffin, the Unicorn, and the Dragon.* Englewood, CO: Libraries Unlimited, 1995.

Rose, Carol. *Giants, Monsters, and Dragons: An Encyclopedia of Folklore, Legend, and Myth.* New York: W. W. Norton, 2000.

Shuker, Dr. Karl. *Dragons: A Natural History*. New York: Simon and Schuster, 1995.

South, Malcolm, ed. *Mythical and Fabulous Creatures: A Sourcebook and Research Guide.* New York: Peter Bedrick Books, 1988.

Notes on Quotations

Chapter 1

p. 9 "The dragon is the largest": Nigg, *Wonder Beasts,* p. 117.

p. 10 "There are diverse sorts": Shuker, *Dragons,* p. 8 (spelling modernized).

p. 11 "There be some dragons": Nigg, *Wonder Beasts,* p. 119.

p. 11 "On my arrival": Gould, *Dragons, Unicorns, and Sea Serpents,* p. 184.

Chapter 2

p. 15 "She cloaked ferocious dragons": Nigg, *The Book of Fabulous Beasts,* p. 21.

p. 18 "fiendish snake, three-jawed": Ingersoll, *Dragons and Dragon Lore,* p. 36.

p. 18 "which devoured men": The Avesta, quoted in Albert J. Carnoy, *Iranian Mythology* (Boston: Marshall Jones Company, 1917), http://rbedrosian.com/carn5.htm

p. 21 "enshrined a great many": Mayor, *The First Fossil Hunters,* p. 130.

Chapter 3

p. 23 "[Various authors] do affirm": Nigg, *Wonder Beasts,* p. 119.

p. 24 "bloated, great she-dragon": Nigg, *The Book of Fabulous Beasts,* p. 35.

p. 24 "His crest was gold": Ovid, *Metamorphoses,* translated by Rolfe Humphries (Bloomington: Indiana University Press, 1955), p. 58.

p. 26 "keen sleepless eyes": South, *Mythical and Fabulous Creatures,* p. 34.

p. 26 "from all his heads": Dobell, *Dragons,* p. 19.

p. 28 "On [the shield's] centre": Gould, *Dragons, Unicorns, and Sea Serpents,* pp. 192–193.

p. 29 "It is deadly": Nigg, *The Book of Fabulous Beasts,* pp. 62–63.

Chapter 4

p. 31 "Come not between": Gould, *Dragons, Unicorns, and Sea Serpents,* p. 192.

p. 31 "The dragon shall [be]": South, *Mythical and Fabulous Creatures,* p. 41.

p. 32 "Then the baleful stranger": *Beowulf,* translated by Charles W. Kennedy, in George K. Anderson and William E. Buckler, eds., *The Literature of England,* 5th ed. (Chicago: Scott, Foresman and Company, 1966), vol. 1, p. 54.

p. 33 "and slit asunder": Ibid., p. 59.

p. 33 "began with ominous signs": Nigg, *The Book of Fabulous Beasts,* p. 152.

p. 34 "Fafnir went up": Snorri Sturluson, *The Prose Edda: Tales from Norse Mythology,* translated by Jean I. Young (Berkeley: University of California Press, 1954), p. 112.

p. 35 "When Fafnir, crawling on his way": Ibid.

p. 36 "As soon as they were near": Geoffrey of Monmouth, *The History of the Kings of Britain,* translated by Lewis Thorpe (New York: Penguin, 1966), p. 171.

p. 37 "with a single beam": Ibid., p. 200.

Chapter 5

p. 39 "And then there was war": Cherry, *Mythical Beasts,* p. 36.

p. 39 "a great red dragon": Ibid.

p. 40 "I saw an angel": Dobell, *Dragons,* p. 10.

p. 40 "the lake of fire": Revelation 20:10 (Revised Standard Version).

p. 43 "he venomed the people": Nigg, *The Book of Fabulous Beasts,* p. 161 (spelling modernized).

p. 44 "rode hardily against the dragon" and "the king was baptized": Ibid., p. 163 (spelling modernized).

Chapter 6

p. 47 "Then Sir Lancelot": South, *Mythical and Fabulous Creatures,* p. 46 (spelling modernized).

p. 48 "He thought he heard": Allan, *The Mythic Bestiary,* p. 126.

p. 50 "eighty yards in length": Ingersoll, *Dragons and Dragon Lore,* p. 39.

p. 51 "Fire sparkles round him": Ibid., p. 40.

Chapter 7

p. 53 "The dragon is the chief": Gould, *Dragons, Unicorns, and Sea Serpents,* p. 398.

p. 54 "Its voice resembles": Ibid., p. 243.

p. 55 "The dragon's skin": Ibid., p. 400.

p. 56 "only seven feet long": Ingersoll, *Dragons and Dragon Lore,* p. 101.
p. 57 "He is the spirit": Ibid., p. 100.

Index

Page numbers for illustrations are in boldface

About the Author

FOX GRADIN, CELESTIAL STUDIOS PHOTOGRAPHY

KATHRYN HINDS grew up near Rochester, New York. She studied music and writing at Barnard College, and went on to do graduate work in comparative literature and medieval studies at the City University of New York. She has written more than forty books for young people, including *Everyday Life in the Roman Empire*, *Everyday Life in the Renaissance*, *Everyday Life in Medieval Europe*, and the books in the series BARBARIANS, LIFE IN THE MEDIEVAL MUSLIM WORLD, LIFE IN ELIZABETHAN ENGLAND, and LIFE IN ANCIENT EGYPT. Kathryn lives in the north Georgia mountains with her husband, their son, and an assortment of cats and dogs. When she is not reading or writing, she enjoys dancing, gardening, knitting, and taking walks in the woods. Visit Kathryn online at www.kathrynhinds.com